making meetings work

PATRICK FORSYTH

Patrick Forsyth runs Touchstone Training & Consultancy, an independent firm based in London that specialises in marketing, sales, and communication skills. He runs both public and tailored in-company courses, and undertakes a wide range of consultancy work from copywriting and brochure design to strategic studies and research. He is the author of a number of successful books on subjects such as sales and marketing, training sessions, time management and successful presentations.

Management Shapers is a comprehensive series covering all the crucial management skill areas. Each book includes the key issues, helpful starting points and practical advice in a concise and lively style. Together, they form an accessible library reflecting current best practice – ideal for study or quick reference.

Other titles in the series:

The Appraisal Discussion
Terry Gillen

Asking Questions
Ian MacKay (second edition)

Assertiveness
Terry Gillen

Constructive Feedback
Roland and Frances Bee

The Disciplinary Interview
Alan Fowler

Leadership Skills
John Adair

Listening Skills (second edition)
Ian MacKay

Motivating People
Iain Maitland

Negotiating, Persuading and Influencing
Alan Fowler

The Selection Interview
Penny Hackett

Working in Teams
Alison Hardingham

The Institute of Personnel and Development is the leading publisher of books and reports for personnel and training professionals, students, and all those concerned with the effective management and development of people at work. For full details of all our titles please contact the Publishing Department:

tel. 0181-263 3387
fax 0181-263 3850
e-mail publish@ipd.co.uk

The catalogue of all IPD titles can be viewed on the IPD website:
http://www.ipd.co.uk

making meetings work

PATRICK FORSYTH

INSTITUTE OF PERSONNEL AND DEVELOPMENT

First published in the *Training Extras* series in 1996

First published in the *Management Shapers* series in 1998

Design by Curve
Typesetting by Paperweight
Printed in Great Britain by
The Guernsey Press, Channel Islands

British Library Cataloguing in Publication Data
A catalogue record for this book is available from the British Library

ISBN
0-85292-765-7

INSTITUTE OF PERSONNEL
AND DEVELOPMENT

IPD House, Camp Road, London SW19 4UX
Tel.: 0181 971 9000 Fax: 0181 263 3333
Registered office as above. Registered Charity No. 1038333.
A company limited by guarantee. Registered in England No. 2931892.

contents

introduction

> Meetings are indispensable when you don't want to do anything.
>
> J. K. Galbraith.

It is said that the ideal meeting is two people – with one absent. If there is one thing in business life that is a mixed blessing, then it is surely meetings.

Yet so much time is spent in them, and so many of them somehow end up being unconstructive, to say the least. Just saying the word 'meeting' is sufficient in some organisations to conjure up a picture of a smoke-filled room, a table covered with papers – and itself covered, in turn, with the rings from coffee mugs – and of wasted time, acrimony, delay, argument, frustration, and decisions not made. How often have you come out of a meeting and not only felt dissatisfied but wondered what you had been doing there at all? If you answer that you never feel like that, then you must work for a truly exceptional organisation; and I am not sure that many people would find it easy to believe you.

Meetings are none the less an important part of organisational communications, consultation, debate and decision-making. We need them, and we need to get the best from them. But we do not need too many, or those that are longer than necessary, or, above all, those that are unconstructive. We need effective meetings – but they do not just happen by themselves. If it is assumed that some deep law of meetings means we must put up with the bad ones in order to get an occasional good one thrown in, then nothing will be done to create a culture of effective meetings. Everyone in an organisation needs actively to work at it. Everyone's role is important, whether they are running a meeting or attending one.

Hence this publication: there are principles and techniques involved. This is no lost cause. It is an area where some consideration, and perhaps also some discipline and cultivation of the right habits, works wonders. Meetings not only *can* be constructive, they *have to* be. Time is just too valuable a resource for us to allow any of it to be frittered away on ineffective meetings. Most organisations have plenty of other things that need to be done – and important things at that.

The cost

Attitude is important here too. How is it that, in many organisations, failures such as an increase in rejection rates in the factory or a drop in sales figures will trigger instant action, whereas the regular exit of people from meetings in muted (and sometimes not so muted) rage, muttering 'What a waste of time!', results only in the setting of the date for the next meeting? The dangers are all too obvious and include meetings that:

- waste time
- waste money
- divert attention from more important tasks
- slow down progress and delay action
- are divisive
- lower morale
- are a platform for the talkative and disruptive
- breed office politics
- create muddle and chaos.

You could doubtless add to the list. Such meetings end up prompting few (or bad) decisions, or simply end in tears.

There are costs involved here, not least of which is opportunity cost. In other words, think about what else could be being done – *achieved* – if people were not in a meeting, and consider how much those other activities might be worth. In an organisation of any size the negative effects of an unconstructive meeting can be multiplied by the number of people involved. That thought is a bit scary. So never say, 'It's just a meeting'; never overlook the costs; aim instead to make sure meetings are productive and useful.

The benefits

Whatever the meeting – large or small, formal or informal, long or short – if it is planned, considered, and conducted with an eye on how it can be made to go well, then it can be made to work.

As has been said, we all need some meetings, yet their role and importance can vary. Meetings are simply a form of communication. They can be used to:

- inform
- analyse and solve problems
- discuss views
- motivate
- reconcile conflict
- obtain feedback
- persuade
- train and develop
- reinforce the *status quo*
- prompt change in knowledge, skills, or attitudes.

Again you can no doubt add to the list. The key role is surely to prompt change (there is no point in having a meeting if everything is going to remain the same); and to do that, decisions must be made. The meeting has therefore to be constructive and put people in a position where good decisions can prompt appropriate action.

It is also worth noting that good meetings are not just useful: most people positively want meetings. Having too few can be as big a mistake as having too many. Why do people want them? There are various reasons. People believe that meetings, for example:

- keep them informed and up to date
- provide individuals with a chance to be both seen and heard
- create involvement with others
- are useful social gatherings
- allow cross-functional contact
- provide individuals with public relations opportunities
- can broaden experience and prompt learning.

And they are right. Meetings are potentially useful. Indeed the progress of an organisation can, in a sense, be certain only if meetings are held and go well.

Enough scene-setting. Let us turn to how to make meetings work. All good meetings need an agenda; the table on page 6 contains ours.

What's next?

We need to consider:

1. ahead of any meeting any relevant matter that can help make it go well
2. how the leadership of a meeting can make a valuable contribution
3. how to be a (successful) participant (although there are lessons here for chairpeople too)
4. the overall dynamics and interactions within meetings
5. last, but not least, what should happen after them.

So, what should we consider before a meeting even begins?

before meetings

If a meeting is to be truly successful then its purpose and content have to be thought through first. The 'I think we're all here, what shall we deal with first?' school of meeting is no good. Making it work starts before the meeting – sometimes long before.

Is your meeting really necessary?

There may be other ways of dealing with the business in hand. So the first question is whether a meeting needs to be called or, if it is not your meeting, needs to be attended. Consider yours first.

Your meetings

The first thing, as with so much in management, is questions. Never just open your mouth and say, 'We had better set a meeting'. Pause and think. Ask yourself: is it a matter for debate or consultation? Or can a decision be made without either of those? Can any information that will be disseminated at the meeting be circulated in any other way? If a brief conversation is all that is necessary, might it not be enough to have a word on the telephone, in the corridor, or over a working lunch? As soon as you ask such questions an alternative often presents itself, and it may well be less time-consuming than a meeting.

Remember that such decisions affect not only your own time. Six people meeting for an hour represent six hours' work time (plus preparing, getting there and ... but you get the point); *this* is the way to think about it. Of course, the more people you invite to a meeting the more this situation multiples; and large meetings tend, by their nature, to last longer than smaller ones.

Other people's meetings

What about meetings called by others? Although there will always be some you have to attend, the principle of 'think first' still applies. You may find there are some you attend for the wrong reasons. For example, it is very easy to find you are really going only to keep in touch or 'just in case something important crops up'. If that is the case then maybe it will be sufficient just to read the minutes. Even if, as a manager, you feel that it is important for your department to be represented you can always delegate someone else to attend and report back.

There may be aspects of a forthcoming meeting that you would enjoy, topics on which your contribution would allow you to shine, but still it may not be a priority to attend. There is an old story, which perhaps illustrates the attitude to take, about a training manager who scheduled a session on delegating skills and sent round a note indicating that certain managers were expected to attend. One promptly replied he would not, but that he would send his assistant! But I digress...

In any case, whatever the meeting is about, make sure it is essential, that there is no alternative, and then read the rest of this chapter before you finalise matters and the meeting gets under way.

Regular meetings

If it is important to consider whether any one meeting is necessary then it is doubly important to consider carefully before getting locked into a series of regular meetings. There are weekly or monthly meetings that continue to be held for no better reason than because they have become a habit. If this is the case then few of them are likely to be useful. Indeed, I would go so far as to want to ban any meeting being prefixed with a word such as 'weekly'.

Admittedly meetings scheduled in advance are usually important. Often it also makes sense to have them on a regular or semi-regular basis. But it may be better to think in terms of, say, 10 a year rather than one a month: regularity may be varied to match the seasonal pattern in a business, with meetings closer or further apart at certain times of year. Get over the problem of getting busy people together by all means, but be warned: this is an area from which stem many unproductive meetings and much waste of time.

A regular meeting can always be cancelled, of course, although I have often heard managers say something like 'Let's let it stand and see what people have to say.' In this (probably well-intentioned) way a manager can earn a reputation for running useless meetings.

But if the meeting is to happen, what will make it effective?

The agenda

Every meeting needs an agenda. In most cases this needs to be in writing and circulated in advance. This is basic, though not often done. A clear agenda can shape and control a meeting in all sorts of ways. It should:

- specify the formalities (do you need to note any apologies for absence, for example?)
- pick up and link points from any previous meetings to ensure continuity
- give people an opportunity to make agenda suggestions
- specify who will lead or contribute to each item
- help individuals to prepare themselves
- order the items for discussion or review; this is something that may need to represent the logical order of the topics, the difficulty they pose (and perhaps the time they will occupy), and the participants' convenience (maybe

someone must leave early and you want something dealt with before this happens)

- reflect any 'hidden' agenda eg with a controversial issue being placed to minimise discussion (just before lunch, say)
- deal with administrative matters such as where and when the meeting will be held and, if it is going to be long, when any breaks or refreshments will come.

Sequence is also important. Selecting a good order in which to go through things can make all the difference. Is, for example, a given item:

- best early on, to get it out of the way while people are fresh
- best placed to provide a link with other items (horses first, carts second)
- the most dependent on preparation
- interesting or important to everyone attending, or to just a few
- in danger of taking too much time and overshadowing other things, or does it have any characteristic – being awkward, unpopular, contentious, or easy, straightforward, quick – that makes it suit a particular placing?

Furthermore, any agenda must be realistic. Ask yourself the following questions:

- Will all the agenda fit within the time available?
- Is there sufficient lead time for notification and preparation?
- Will one major item put the rest of the meeting in jeopardy?
- Are items matched to participants? (Are the right people going to be there – or not?)
- Is the style of meeting right? (Training or persuasion may take longer than information-giving, for example.)

It is too late to do anything about it if you find out only after your meeting that the way it was set up is preventing it from operating effectively.

Check the overall look and balance of an agenda to make sure that you are not attempting too much in the time available. If patience runs out things will end up taking longer, or will not have justice done to them. Above all, the agenda should reflect the objectives of the meeting. (Indeed a full agenda may sometimes address *why* something is being tabled as well as the plain fact that it is.) Before going any further, therefore, we turn to objectives.

Why are we meeting?

Sometimes meetings do not become ineffective because of how they proceed: they are doomed from the start because they do not have clear, specific objectives. Do *not* meet in order to:

- start the planning process
- discuss cost savings
- review training needs
- improve administration.

Set clear, explicit objectives. Avoid vaguely worded items such as 'discuss reducing expenditure'; say instead that you want 'to decide how to reduce the advertising budget by 10 per cent over the next six months.' If objectives are clear it will help in a number of specific ways:

- People will understand why the meeting is taking place.
- They will be better able, and perhaps more inclined, to prepare.
- The discussion will be more focused.
- The proceedings will be easier to control.

The net result is that the meeting is more likely to achieve its aims.

Time and timing

In a busy world time is always of the essence; here we deal with several aspects of it with regard to meetings.

Starting time

Basics first: every meeting needs a starting time. Exactly when that is can affect what subsequently happens. Do you want a meeting that lasts just an hour? If so, then 12 noon or 4pm are good times: the meeting will not drag on if people want to get to lunch or go home. Equally a meeting at 8.30am may give you an uninterrupted hour before most of the distractions of the day start to crowd in.

Choose your time well and then stick to it. This may sound simple, but it needs some thought and resolve.

Respect for time

This is fundamentally important. Nothing is guaranteed to get a meeting off to a worse start, with everyone in a bad mood, than the consequences of poor timekeeping. Imagine the scene: people congregate, it is time to start the meeting, but not everyone is present. It is decided to 'give them five minutes'. Coffee is poured. Various *ad hoc* (and probably not very useful) discussions start. Time passes and finally the meeting starts 15 minutes late with one person still to arrive. Ten minutes later, just as things are getting down to business, the latecomer arrives. Apologies and bringing the latecomer up to date waste another five minutes, and so on, and so on… The greater the number of people attending the meeting, the greater the waste and irritation.

So always start meetings on time. It is worth repeating: *always start meetings on time*. Doing so may be difficult at first, but the only way to crack the problem is to instil habits and respect. If someone is late, say so! Try not to recapitulate (do it one-to-one at the end, perhaps). Be consistent. Let the word go round: 'You'd better not be late for one of Patrick's meetings!' It really is worth the effort. Human nature being what it is, you will not succeed 100 per cent with everyone, but this is no reason to give up and admit defeat. It is worth persisting, because the attitudes struck here are highly beneficial – and perhaps to more than simply the efficiency of a meeting.

Finishing time

Every meeting should have not only a starting time but a finishing time also. It is a courtesy to people (and helps keep the meeting on track) to set aside a specific time for a session. Although you can always finish early, you should try not to overrun. The more you do this the better you will get at judging how much time things are likely to take.

A timed agenda

Similarly it helps to have items on the agenda timed (perhaps not every last one, but certainly the main topics). Again this helps focus discussion and will give you something to aim for – 'Let's try to sort this out in the next 15 minutes.' It really does help.

The people

Once you have a clear objective and agenda you can consider the people who should or should not attend. Generally speaking the more who are present, the longer things will take. Think about:

- who has to be there
- who should observe
- who might find it useful
- who has something positive to contribute
- who has an axe to grind
- who will make unnecessary problems and dilute effectiveness.

The job is to assemble the right group in a considered manner, matching expertise with the topic to be discussed. Beware of the wrong influences: office politics, favours, democracy, and social factors, for instance. The group must be able to make whatever decisions are necessary and everyone present should have a clear and positive reason for being there. You also need to think about who will do what. Who will be ' in the chair' (more on this later)? Who will take notes, act as secretary or, afterwards, prepare the minutes? Key roles need deciding in advance, right down to who will organise the tea and coffee.

A final point here: one aspect of pre-meeting preparation (more of this for both chair and participants in Chapters 2 and 3) that may be necessary is pre-meeting meetings. This is, I hope, not double Dutch but a way of describing the getting together in twos, threes or whatever to plan joint strategies so as to act in accord on the day. Such preliminaries can have a powerful effect on the way a meeting runs. This may be positive or negative; sometimes such sessions will make a meeting shorter and more constructive; on other occasions they can represent attempts at manipulation. Whichever is the case it is important:

- never to underestimate the importance of pre-meeting preparation or assume others will not be doing it
- to take time yourself to form the necessary alliances
- to watch for signs of other such alliances and anticipate their effect on the meeting.

Bear in mind also that both visible and invisible alliances can be useful, although some that are *thought* to be invisible may well be revealed come the day.

The meeting environment

Everything – even the room and location – acts in some way to influence how a meeting will go. The hazards are many and include:

- too many people in too small a room
- too much smoke
- too little light
- uncomfortable chairs
- no visual aids when these would be useful [1]
- interruptions, which can range form a badly timed tea break (ie one that happens just as things are starting to flow) to the now ubiquitous mobile phone (insist they are switched off).

Some thought is necessary if such factors are to be avoided. Plan to hold your meeting in the right place, with the right surroundings and equipment – 'right' meaning anything that will act positively to make sure things go well. Choose, for example, somewhere:

- quiet (if possible, without a telephone)
- private (if necessary)
- with sufficient space
- with the required number of power points
- with comfortable chairs
- with a good, well-ventilated atmosphere
- with a pleasant ambience (this is not necessarily a luxury

– people will be less able to think creatively if they are unhappy with their surroundings).

There is an old military saying that time spent in reconnaissance is seldom wasted. So too with the preliminaries dealt with in this chapter. Meetings are important. A great deal can depend on their going well – everything from reputations to large amounts of money. It is therefore important to create a sound foundation for the meeting process.

There are major factors here, such as agendas and objectives; these are not helped if details are missed, and someone disappears from a meeting 'to get a pencil' just as it starts.

What's next?

Next on our agenda is the question of who is in the chair, and how this helps to ensure a constructive meeting.

Endnote

1 This is not the place for a review of the relative merits of, say, overhead projectors *vs* flipcharts, but do remember that running certain meetings without appropriate equipment is very difficult. People may spend several minutes trying to grasp the implications of some figures, for instance, whereas a pie chart on a screen would have everyone get to grips with them in a moment.

2 leading meetings

Somewhere in Shakespeare's *Much Ado About Nothing* there is the line 'When two men ride of a horse, one must sit behind.' So it is with meetings: even with the less formal ones, someone has to be in charge. That does *not* imply that whoever is 'in the chair' should be the most senior person present or should do most of (or even lead) the talking. What it does imply is that he or she should be responsible for directing the meeting.

Every meeting should therefore have a 'chair' (though they may need no official tag). An appropriate person is needed, because the role is important and may be substantial. Don't choose just anyone – 'You lead, John: Mary did it last time we met.' An effectively conducted chairing role can ensure a well-directed meeting, which can in turn mean that:

- the meeting will focus better on its objectives
- discussion can be more constructive
- a thorough review can be ensured so that *ad hoc* decisions are avoided
- all sides of the argument or case can be reflected upon and weighed in the balance

- proceedings can be kept businesslike and less argumentative (even when dealing with contentious issues).

As we can see, all the results of effective chairing are positive and likely to make for an equally effective meeting. Put succinctly, a good chairperson will lead the meeting, handle the discussion, and see that objectives are met – promptly, efficiently, effectively and without wasting time.

The right person

As has been said, this is an important role. The choice of who exactly will be in the chair must reflect the responsibilities that the task entails. Steps need to be taken from the beginning to get a suitable person in the chair, and to get participants to accept the *need* for someone to be in charge – to see it as something practical that will help everyone. To state the obvious, an ordered meeting will be likely to achieve more than one where chaos reigns.

At this point it is appropriate to refer to two key rules that any chairperson must stick to (and which any group of people meeting should respect). They are, very simply:

- Only one person at a time may talk.
- The chairperson decides who (should this be necessary).

Already this should begin to make you think about who will make a good chairperson. The following check-list of responsibilities lays out the full picture.

The leader's responsibilities

The list that follows illustrates the range and nature of the tasks involved. It also shows clearly that there are genuine skills involved, skills that must perhaps be studied, learned, and practised. Whoever is chairing the meeting must:

- command the respect of those attending (and if he or she does not know them, then such respect must be won rapidly by the way he or she is seen to operate)
- come prepared (ie having read any relevant documents and taken any other action necessary in order to be able to take charge – and he or she should also encourage others to do the same, because good preparation makes for more considered and succinct contributions to the meeting)
- be on time
- start on time
- ensure that any administrative matters are taken care of appropriately (eg refreshments, taking minutes)
- start on the right note and lead smoothly into the agenda

- introduce people if necessary (and therefore know the names of all those attending – name cards can help everyone at some meetings)
- set, and keep, the rules
- control the discussion, and do so in light of the different kinds of people who may be present (the talkative, the strident etc)
- encourage contributions where appropriate or necessary
- ask questions to clarify matters where necessary (it is important to query straight away anything unclear in order to save time and arguments – if the meeting runs on with something being misinterpreted it will become a muddle, and a conclusion will take longer to reach
- ensure that everyone has his or her say
- act to keep the discussion to the point
- listen (if the chair has missed things then the chances of the meeting proceeding smoothly are slim, and it may deteriorate into 'But-you-said' arguments)
- watch the clock, remind others to do the same, and manage time pressure
- summarise the discussion clearly, succinctly, and at regular intervals
- cope with upsets, outbursts, and high emotion

- provide the final word by summarising and bringing matters to a conclusion (including any final administrative detail such as setting the date for the next action or for a further meeting)
- see to any follow-up action (especially important when there is a series of meetings, in order to avoid having people promise something at one and turn up at the next having done little or nothing).

All this must be done with patience, goodwill, good humour, and respect not only for all those present (and maybe others) but also for the objectives of the meeting. Now let us turn to a number of points worth investigating in more detail.

Getting off to a good start

The best meetings start well, continue well, and end well. A good start helps set the scene, and this too is the responsibility of whoever is in the chair. It works best to start the meeting in a way that:

- is positive
- makes its purpose (and procedure) clear
- establishes the chairperson's authority and right to be in charge
- creates the right atmosphere (which may differ depending on whether it is to prompt creative thinking or, say, detailed analysis of figures)

- generates interest and enthusiasm for what is to come (yes, even if it is seen as tedious regular review)
- is immediately perceived as businesslike.

It may also help if the chairperson involves others early on, rather than beginning with a lengthy monologue; which takes us to the next point.

Prompting discussion

Of course, there are meetings where *prompting* contributions is the least of the chairperson's problems. But if you are in the chair you will want contributions from everyone (why otherwise did you invite them?). So, to ensure that you get adequate and representative discussion, and to ensure that subsequent decisions are made on all the appropriate facts and information, you may need to prompt discussion.

Sometimes there are specific reasons why meeting participants hold back. They may for example:

- fear rejection
- feel pressure from other, more senior, or more powerful, people
- lack preparation
- have an incomplete understanding of what has gone before.

Indeed they may simply lack any encouragement to make contributions. A good chairperson will ask for views, and do so in a way that prompts open, considered comments. But note that it is sometimes easy to skew comments (wittingly or not) by the tone or manner with which they are called for. For instance, a senior manager is unlikely to encourage creative suggestions if he or she fields a personal thought first, as though he or she were saying, 'It is only a suggestion, but bear in mind who's making it.' Be careful not to load the dice in this way.

Much comment-prompting will come through questions.

Questioning techniques

Questions must of course be clear. There are two kinds of question: open, and closed.

Open questions

These cannot be answered with a simple 'yes' or 'no'. The kind of open questions that work best start with 'what', 'why', or 'how' or may be introduced with a phrase such as 'Tell me about ...' or 'What do you think about ...?' They get people talking rather than elicit a monosyllabic reply.

Closed questions

This kind is useful when you want *not* to encourage more talk. Closed questions *can* be answered with a simple 'yes' or 'no' or in some equally brief manner (eg if the question is

'Who could help provide that information?').

The circumstances will dictate how questions are best asked. Discussion can be prompted around the meeting in more complex ways. The table below shows six different ways.

Six ways of promoting inputs

Overhead questions
These are put to the meeting as a whole and left for whoever picks them up. They are useful for starting discussion.

Overhead directed questions
These also are put to the whole meeting. Unlike the overhead question described above, however, you ask the question a second time directly to an individual; or, after a pause to overcome any lack of response, you can use an open question such as 'Now, what do we all think about this? ... David?'

Questions direct to an individual
These are *not* first put to the whole meeting, and are useful to get an individual reaction to check understanding.

Rhetorical questions
These demand no answer. They can be a good way to make a point or prompt thinking; and the chairperson can always provide a response if he or she wishes. Useful?

Redirected questions
Here a question directed to the chairperson is redirected to the meeting either as an overhead or direct question: 'Good question. What do we all think? Mary?'

Development questions
These really get discussion going. They build on the answer to an earlier question and move it round the meeting: 'So, David thinks it will take too long. Are there any other problems?'

Prompting discussion is as important as control. It is the only way of making sure the meeting is well balanced and takes in all required points of view. If decisions are made in the absence of this, someone may be back to you later saying something like, 'This is not really acceptable. My department never really got a chance to make their case.'

For this reason it may sometimes be necessary to persevere in order to get all the comment that the meeting needs. Ways have to be found to achieve this. Two examples are:

- *Asking again*. It is as simple as that. Rephrase the question (perhaps it was not understood the first time) and ensure both that the point is clear and that people know comment *is* required.
- *Using silence*. It is true that silence can be embarrassing. But even a short silence to make it clear you will wait for an answer may be sufficient to get someone speaking. So do not rush on; after all, the point deserves a moment's thought.

This is an important area, and it may be worth your while to investigate further: another publication in this series, *Asking Questions*, by Ian MacKay (IPD, 1995), makes a useful and manageable source of reference.

Concentration

A good, serious meeting demands concentration. It is the job of whoever is in the chair to assist in achieving this both in themselves and in others. Beware interruptions. Make sure you know how to deal with messages ('Excuse me a moment – I really must deal with this one'), mobile telephones, or simply the refreshments arriving. All of these can delay proceedings and ensure that concentration is lost. It therefore helps if:

- rules are laid down about messages
- breaks are organised (for longer sessions) to let people deal with messages etc; they should be not too long or too frequent, so that participants do not lose concentration on the meeting
- an appropriate time for refreshments is organised in advance (or they can be taken after the meeting)
- others outside the meeting (including switchboard operators and secretaries) are briefed as to how matters should be handled. It is as bad – perhaps worse – for a key customer, say, to be told, 'Sorry, they're in a meeting', as for the meeting itself to be interrupted; so decide your priority.

If there are unforeseen interruptions then do not compete with them while people's attention is elsewhere. Wait, deal with them, and then continue, recapping if necessary.

Concentration is vital and, of course, needs to be focused on the right things within the meeting. Do not be sidetracked. Beware of digressions. Beware also of running a meeting within a meeting: sometimes you will unearth separate issues that are worth noting, but that should be pursued or investigated on some other occasion.

Disorder and disruption

Sometimes even the best-planned and organised meetings get out of hand. We shall touch on this again in Chapter 4, but here it is worth noting some key rules for the chairperson:

- Never get upset or emotional yourself.
- Isolate one element of what is being expressed and try to deal with that in a way that reduces the overall temperature of the debate.
- Agree (at least with the sentiments) before regrouping – 'you're right: this is a damned difficult issue and emotions are bound to run high. Now let's take one thing at a time … .'

If these approaches do not work you may have to take more drastic action, such as:

- calling for a few minutes' complete silence before attempting to move on
- calling a short break – and insist that it is taken with no

further discussion of the heated issue

- ▲ putting the problem item to one side until later (though be sure to specify how and when it will be dealt with – and make sure you do what was agreed)
- ● abandoning the meeting until another time.

Abandoning a meeting is clearly a last resort, but as such may be better than allowing disorder to continue. Usually a firm stand as soon as any sort of unrest occurs will meet the problem head on and deal with it. Whatever happens, as it says in Douglas Adams' *Hitchhikers' Guide to the Universe*: don't panic!

I would not want to give the impression that chairing meetings is all drama, however, so let us end this chapter with something more constructive.

Sparking creativity

It is said that whereas managers are not paid to have all the good ideas needed to keep their department (or whatever) running effectively, they *are* paid to make sure there are sufficient ideas to keep it ahead. As a result many meetings need to be creative. Two heads really can be better than one. Yet new ideas can also prompt a negative cycle all too easily. Such discussion can spiral into a tit for tat of 'your idea's no good' or 'mine's better' – with scoring points taking precedence over giving new ideas a chance.

This is another thing that the chairperson has to deal with: he or she needs to foster creative thinking and openmindedness to ensure that instant negative reactions do not become the order of the day. The chairperson must therefore:

- actively stimulate creative thinking (and he or she should clearly say that this is part of the meeting, and rule against anyone who instantly rejects ideas without first considering them)
- personally contribute new ideas or steer the discussion in new, or unusual, directions
- find new ways of looking at things
- consider novel approaches and give them a chance
- aim to solve problems, not tread familiar pathways.

Some groups who meet regularly get better and better at this. But this does not usually happen spontaneously; more often it is the result of someone putting together the right team and prompting them not only to think along certain lines but also always to remain open-minded above all.

We shall return to some of these issues. Here let us conclude by stressing again the influence of the choice of the chairperson, the nature of that role and the way it is carried out. Without someone at the helm, any meeting risks running onto the rocks.

What's next?

In the next chapter we shall look at the question of attending meetings: what, as a participant, can you contribute to, and get from, meetings? There are even more lessons here for you if you are normally in the chair.

attending meetings

Meetings can waste time, money, and effort – not least *your* time, money, and effort. But the benefits of a good meeting in terms of ideas, debate, decision, and communication are considerable, as has already been mentioned. Perhaps we should all resolve never to go to a meeting unless we are convinced that it is likely to be genuinely constructive and useful. Specifically, you must ask yourself every time a meeting beckons:

- What can I contribute?
- What can I get from it?

Come to definite answers to both questions. This means considering alternatives: instead of going yourself, can you submit a note, read the minutes afterwards, or delegate someone else to attend? Make a conscious decision about attending: unless there is a three-line whip, make sure you really feel it is necessary.

Effective participation

Once you have decided to attend you can consider how to make doing so worthwhile. After all, meetings are no exception to the old saying that you only get out of things what you put in. Overall, the key things that make for effective participation in meetings are:

- *sound preparation*. You have to know what will be discussed, be ready for it, and have done your homework.
- *effective communication*. You have to judge well what you say and how you say it.
- *well-handled discussion*. You have to be not only ready to make prepared contributions but also to think quickly on your feet in order to respond appropriately to the contributions of others; in other words, you have to be able to put your case effectively not just in isolation but so that it surfaces through what may be a maelstrom of comment.

One other point is worth a short digression: you may need to look the part. Although I would not presume to tell you how to dress, you may be involved in circumstances where this needs a moment's thought. Perhaps you are to attend a meeting where not everyone will know you, for example, or perhaps there is some other factor that will make your appearance especially important. If you rush in late, unkempt, and clutching a collapsing pile of files you will certainly not give the desired impression. You could do worse than to consider the impression you want to make: presumably, that of someone who is well prepared, efficient, authoritative, expert, well informed, and credible. You can compile your own version of such a list: you know what is important in your own circles or organisation.

Seating is important in the same regard. Do not try to command a meeting from round a corner or out on a limb; sit where you can be seen and from where you can communicate effectively. (If it is your meeting, give some forethought to the seating – would a round table work well for some meetings?)

Sound preparation

Ensuring that you get the right message over needs some thought and well-considered action. This starts, unsurprisingly, with preparation. The first rule is simple: always prepare. You will never make your point well if you try to do so off the top of your head. The second rule is: horses for courses. Meetings vary and the amount of preparation you need to do will vary likewise (and will not necessarily relate directly to, say, the length of the meeting). Sometimes preparation requires only a couple of minutes' thought, sometimes a day's work (and everything in between). The key areas involved here include the need to:

- read anything necessary *in advance*. This might include past minutes, agendas, documents, reports, and memos that have been circulated and have a bearing on the meeting. It might also include background reading or research to familiarise yourself with a topic (perhaps with the aim to do so better than other participants).
- annotate any relevant documents and make your own notes as necessary. It is essential to be able to check facts

fast at a meeting. You do not impress people by fumbling through a pile of papers, saying, 'I know it is here somewhere.'

- note who will attend so that your plans take into account their roles and positions. For example, is anyone coming on whom you can rely for support – or is it yours that will be relied on?
- plan questions that you will need to ask as the meeting progresses. Sometimes you may need to plan exactly how you will ask them.
- prepare your contribution. This is necessary when the situation is more formal (it may be almost like a presentation). Make sure that you have thought things through and have any necessary notes of what you need to say and how you will put it over.

In general make *notes* of anything you will need to know, say, or do. It is no good trusting to your memory and then coming out of the meeting saying, 'I just wish I had said ...'.

On the day all sorts of difficulties can conspire to make what you want to do more difficult. People may not listen as attentively as you want (and, no doubt, feel you deserve); they may stick doggedly to their current views and the *status quo*, and find it difficult to be convinced by your arguments. There may also be any number of other pressures; time constraints, an emergency of some kind, or other issues might arise that threaten to thwart your intentions.

All of this goes to prove our point: preparation is key, and time spent on it can make all the difference between a good meeting and a complete waste of time. It is important to get it right: many meetings have a great deal riding on them.

Controlling your nerves

However well you have prepared for your meeting, you are unlikely to succeed in your intentions if (as we have already said) you fail to communicate successfully during it. Before looking in detail at the principles involved in getting your point across, it is worth mentioning something that can derail you at the start: nerves. Meetings can be daunting occasions, all the more so if they are especially important, if you are the most junior person there, or if you have to stand up and make a formal presentation. The additional factors involved in presentations are unfortunately beyond our brief here.

Once again preparation is the best antidote for nerves: you'll feel less nervous if you are clear about what you want to say and do. Simple practical measures may also be useful, ranging from a deep breath to a sip of water. 'Stage fright' is not, however, entirely negative: the adrenalin produces a stimulus that can be useful.

Effective communication

There are occasions when the desire to transfer information is frustrated by the circumstances, which compounds problems and puts recipients in danger of failing to perceive your point. Let me rephrase that: communication is not easy.

Never assume it is easy. Always think about the best way to make even a seemingly simple point. It was ex-President Richard Nixon who is usually credited with the remark, 'I know you believe you understand what you think I said, but I am not sure you realise that what you heard is not what I meant.' There is a serious point here, and I suspect you do not need to have attended many meetings to have seen poor communication in action.

There are several factors here that should be considered if communication at a meeting is to work well.

Stick to the rules

Following a few basic rules will help you and everyone else present (at least they will prevent the meeting from deteriorating into a shouting match). So do not:

- monopolise the conversation
- constantly interrupt others
- become emotional or argumentative to no good purpose
- make it difficult to stick to the allotted time
- appear unprepared, undisciplined, or a troublemaker
- digress pointlessly from the topic.

Try to use the chairperson and any agreed procedure in order to play your part in creating an orderly meeting.

It is, however, said that rules are made to be broken, and although it may be very much the exception to break them, there are occasions when the best tactic is to do just that, for example to use one of the following in a calculated way to make a point:

- a dramatic outburst
- a fist banged on the table as you say 'No!'
- a display of emotion
- some humour
- bad temper (though it must be *controlled*)
- an interruption (to cause a delay, perhaps).

Do not overdo it, or such tactics will quickly become self-defeating.

Stick to the structure

Often a meeting proceeds along lines dictated by the chairperson or simply according to practicality. A useful sequence is:

- *introduction*: stating the reason for a given item, setting the scene, referring back to previous discussion, and spelling out the sub-agenda for the item
- *setting out the issues*: putting points for and against, outlining key points (eg costs, timing, staffing etc),

putting both the main issues and any implications

- *debate*: developing other contributions into logical arguments and establishing for everyone there a basis upon which decisions can be made
- *summary*: a pulling together of previous discussion and a look ahead to future action, communication, or decisions.

This structure usually makes a good way to proceed. You can usefully take this to the point of labelling your intentions, saying, for example, 'Let me summarise …' or 'Let me just comment on the costs issue …' to make clear what you are doing, and perhaps effectively reserve the right to come back on other points.

Get your facts right

Perhaps this should go without saying, but meetings can spend an inordinately long time querying, checking, or challenging facts. Where information proves incorrect, credibility can collapse (even, in fact, if the actual *fact* was not key). This means you must take time to check, check, and check again. It also means that you must put information over in a way that is:

- *explicit*: state things plainly, without obscuring them with irrelevancies
- *accurate*: make sure your information is exactly right

- *precise*: choose well just the right piece of information to make the point.

This does not, I hope, sound pedantic. It matters, and an example may make clear how. Take figures. Say a cost is quoted as being 'up 9.2 per cent', but that this proves inaccurate. Saying afterwards that you meant '*about* 9 per cent' is too late: credibility will have been diluted just a bit – maybe an important bit. This is an area for considerable care.

Always observe

Never get so set on what you are trying to say that you forget to note what others in the meeting are doing. After all, your comments will have to be fine-tuned in the light of your understanding of the state of the meeting. Take care to:

- *watch* everything that goes on. See how people are reacting to the meeting (and to you) in their gestures and expressions – both are an important element of overall communications. Sometimes information available this way is subtle, or it may be more dramatic – with a loud snore from your left meaning that whoever is speaking has not succeeded in generating the desired interest or enthusiasm.
- *listen* attentively and actively. Make notes. Be seen to be listening. And never allow the chairperson to respond to you by saying, 'If you had been listening earlier, then...'.

You will be able to make your points well only if you are in touch with the feeling of the meeting – constantly and accurately.

Well-handled discussion

In communications terms there are a number of things to achieve when you open your mouth at a meeting. You want people to listen, believe what you say is relevant, and ultimately be prompted to agree or take action on a basis that reflects your views. Thus what you say needs to be understandable, attractive, and credible. Although these need to come over in a cohesive way, they are worth reviewing separately first.

Make what you say understandable

The difficulties on this point have already been referred to. Here we note a number of mechanisms that help to make sure that what you say is truly understood:

- *Use clear signposts*. In other words, tell people in advance how you will deal with something. (This is, incidentally, what I have just done by saying above that the key aims were to make what is said understandable, attractive and credible, then taking them one at a time.) If people are clear about what is coming up, they are more likely to want to listen. The same applies to subpoints, which can be presented with more signposting. You cannot really have too much of it.

- *Have a clear structure*. This is always important, even for brief remarks. The logic must be clear: a beginning, a middle, and an end are helpful. Whatever precise structure you choose, it must be appropriate – and signposted.
- *Use the right sequence*. This may take any form you like, for example one relating to chronological events, but again it should be spelt out and chosen to work sensibly for you.
- *Use visual aids*. A picture really can be worth a thousand words. The time taken to produce a chart, diagram, graph or whatever is well worthwhile (you then have to decide how to use it – as a slide, handout, or displayed on a simple flipchart).
- *Avoid jargon*. Or rather, use it carefully. It can be useful. It abbreviates and is only what we might call 'professional slang'. But it can also confuse, especially if you misjudge the level of technicality that is appropriate for a group. It needs watching because the use of jargon can become a reflex action – sometimes you don't know you're doing it.
- *Avoid gobbledegook*. Nobody will take you seriously if you say 'Considerable progress has been made in the preliminary work directed towards the establishment of the starting-point and initial activities', if what you mean is simply 'We are still trying to decide how to begin.' Nor should you speak of 'this moment in time' when

you mean 'now' or start every other sentence with the word 'Basically ...'.

Remember, if you are not understood, nothing else will matter. Although few will agree with something they do not understand, in meetings many are reluctant actually to say 'I don't understand' for fear that it is they who are being dense, so you will not always get feedback to allow correction. Create understanding as the foundation of everything else you do, and you are off to a good start.

Make what you say attractive

It will be clear even to those with minimal experience of meetings that there is much more to them than simply telling people things: they will often need *persuading*. Indeed they may need motivating, filling with enthusiasm, and more. This involves a whole area of skill that goes beyond this book but that is dependent on two key intentions. You must:

- identify the needs of others and try to see things from their point of view. If you understand their perspective you will be better placed to anticipate their objections and see what is likely to persuade them.
- put over a case that reflects this understanding and shows the others specifically, and if necessary individually, how yours will be better.

This subject is covered in another book in the Management Shapers series (Alan Fowler's *Negotiating, Persuading and*

Influencing, IPD, 1995). Here let me just repeat that you should not believe you are there simply to tell people things – you are in fact doing something that is inherently more complex, and should be prepared to act accordingly.

Make what you say credible

It is axiomatic that just saying 'I say so' is not often likely to carry the day (unless you outrank the group in every way). You need to add credibility to a case by injecting evidence or proof from elsewhere. This can be done in a number of ways, for example by using:

- figures and statistics
- concrete examples
- something visual or descriptive
- the results of a test or trial
- expert or objective comment from elsewhere (including from outside the organisation)
- something in writing
- research.

You need to think about where you will need to produce your proof, what will serve the purpose, and how to put it over.

Before we discuss the dynamics of meetings (in Chapter 4), there are two more things to consider in order to communicate effectively in, and get the most out of, meetings.

Timing your remarks

Deciding when to speak is worth a moment's thought – but there are no infallible rules. Make a point too early, and it may be forgotten by the end of the meeting; leave it too late, and the end of the meeting comes before you have a chance to make it. A few guidelines may help:

- Do not prepare to speak in a way that will fit only at a particular moment. Fate will decree that the situation will not be as you imagine; remain flexible.
- Consider your comments not in isolation, but in the context of the other views being, or likely to be, expressed.
- Play to your strengths: are you best at introducing, developing, or summarising an argument?
- Make your future intentions clear. Reserve the right to make a further comment later: 'I have some thoughts about costs, too; perhaps I can come back to that later in the agenda.'

The worst mistake is leaving things too late. If you perpetually wait for some imagined 'best moment' it may never come, and you may end up either not making your point or else making it, by default, at a bad moment.

Finally, how should you approach all this?

The right attitude

Meetings demand *active* participation. You have ever to be on your toes, with your wits about you, ready to contribute in a considered, fine-tuned way as the meeting progresses. It helps if you:

- remain alert and concentrate on everything that is going on throughout the process (even if some things are of less interest to you)
- listen – carefully – to everything that is said and make notes as necessary
- observe what others are up to, how they are reacting, and plan in the light of this
- keep thinking – and always engage the brain before the mouth whenever you speak
- remain calm and collected, whatever the provocation and however far from your anticipated vision of the meeting it strays.

There is a lot to think about here. You have to bear in mind several of the factors commented on in this chapter simultaneously. Individually they are mostly plain common sense, but orchestrating them is complex.

What's next?

We shall look at what can produce both greater complications and opportunities – the dynamics and interactions inherent in meetings.

the dynamics of meetings

Meetings do not only involve people individually. There are dynamics involved in the way a group works. It is said (cynically) that a meeting is a gathering of people who singly can do nothing, but together can decide that nothing can be done. The reverse should be true. Meetings are there to make things happen, and part of what happens does so in a way that cannot be duplicated by one person working on their own. Something is created by the interaction of individuals, by debate, consultation, and the sharing of ideas and experience. Or rather it can be.

It has already been said that people must come to a meeting open-minded. More than this, it helps if everyone comes with a constructive belief that the meeting can be made to work, can be creative, and is going to come up with solutions or ideas. This means in turn that participants accept that working together can be difficult. They need to work actively to remove those difficulties as a preliminary to a useful meeting and both encourage and use positive group dynamics to make things work well.

In this chapter we shall consider one or two examples of group dynamics, link them to the power of discussion, and see how different styles of approach influence events. First let us consider a couple of group aspects of meetings.

Social factors

All organisations have a social structure, or rather a number of interlocking social structures. They feed on contact and communications, for which meetings provide an opportunity. Although it is easy to have too many meetings, an organisation that had none would be a very sterile environment.

Meetings must have an objective and stick to it. But it is fruitless to think that other interactions stop just because we are working down an agenda. People want to meet, to exchange information (and gossip) and, more positively, update their knowledge and extend their experience. Team aspects must be superimposed on this general picture. If it is a team meeting, then (all being well) those attending will positively want to get together; but if more than one team is involved, rivalries may show themselves and get in the way of smooth business.

Some of the negative aspects can be reduced by both the chairperson and each individual (who can for instance resolve to keep the gossip in check or meet one or two people just ahead of the main meeting). But it may also be necessary to accommodate the social side to some extent rather than fight it – better to reduce it substantially and do so amicably than try to stamp it out and upset people. To give an example:

I was recently asked to run a course for an organisation starting at 10am, later than is normal. The late start was because the gathering time was 9am: as the managing director explained, 'They meet up very rarely and the social side is important. If they get it out of their system at the beginning they will work that much harder thereafter.' An interesting thought to ponder.

Motivation

A good meeting can and should be motivational (motivation being maintained by many and disparate influences). It is worth thinking about those factors that can be used to increase the motivation of a group as they meet. For example, motivation will be higher if:

- everyone understands the purpose of the meeting
- there are no major conflicts between individual and group intentions
- there are no 'passengers'
- there is trust and respect for the chairperson
- team members are loyal to one another
- there is prior experience of working successfully together
- there is no destructive politics at work
- confidence is felt that the right team has been assembled

- hierarchy does not interfere with debate, eg by restricting free comment.

Sometimes there are real contradictions that cannot be avoided, for example individuals having to come to terms with something that will work for the group but be inconvenient for them. But a well-motivated group will obviously work better than one whose motivation is low. If the factors listed above can be accommodated as much as possible, so much the better.

The right amount of discussion

Throughout this text discussion has been labelled a 'good thing'; and so it is – up to a point. Too little, and the subject is not properly reviewed; too much, and the meeting goes on interminably with points being made that add little to the sum of points already on the table. It is useful to weigh up just how much discussion is going to be useful; the box opposite sets out some pros and cons.

People

It would be a funny old world, it is said, if we were all the same. But we are not, and one consequence of this is that meetings can suffer from a mismatch of personal styles. The first time to think about this is when you are considering who should come to a meeting although, to be realistic, what you may see as unfortunate combinations are sometimes inevitable. So here we shall consider practical ways of dealing with difficult people.

Discussion check-list

Excessive discussion may mean:

- too many alternatives or too much detail to handle at one time
- too much emotion
- more frequent misunderstandings
- the emergence of opposing sides
- more time being taken to reach conclusions, or no conclusion being reached
- digressions on minor issues
- lack of attention to detail
- circular arguments
- drift into a lack of realism
- repetition
- boredom
- undue attention to detail – nitpicking.

Restricted discussion may mean:

- withholding key information
- overhasty decisions
- disorganised follow-up action
- no real commitment to decisions taken
- decisions not supported later
- stalemate (with people digging their heels in, when fuller debate might have reached agreement more easily)
- low morale and lack of enthusiasm
- fixation with the past.

The talkative

These are often show-offs who want attention, but they may also be enthusiasts for certain topics, which is good. They may alternatively be aiming to monopolise the conversation in order to overpower others' views and so get their own way.

Solution The first job is to get a word in. Pounce on any pause (even just a breath!) and call a halt to the flow of words, ideally with a positive comment such as a word of thanks. Then move on, selecting a new starting-point or throwing the ball to someone else. You can ask the group a general question such as 'What do others think of that point?' or a more specific one such as 'What David has said raises the question of timing; what do we have to say about that?' The job here is to avoid talkative people wasting others' time, while ensuring that you do get the core of good points they may have to make.

The gusher

This kind of person is worse than the talkative because he or she has more sinister motives, being intent on drowning others out and getting his or her own point over to the exclusion of others.

Solution The timed agenda and good discipline will help here. Otherwise it is again necessary to interrupt, perhaps to summarise or to focus on just one thing the gusher has said: 'Before you go on, let me see if I understood what you are saying about Stage One. You think …'. Control the gusher carefully when he or she rejoins the debate.

The sphinx

Silent people also present problems, especially if you know they do have something to contribute. The reasons for their silence may range from shyness to boredom or indifference.

Solution Asking questions (and waiting for an answer) is the best tactic here. An easy comment may be requested first to get them talking, followed by requests for more detail. If someone is holding back for reasons other than those mentioned above, a more direct approach may be necessary: 'You have a lot of experience with this, what do you think?' (And yes, a little flattery may help.)

Separate meeters

Whispered conversations as the meeting proceeds are distracting for everyone. They may, however, be constructive or negative.

Solution Pausing isolates the chatter and draws attention to it (often this is sufficient to stop it). Then you can identify what is going on, find out whether it is relevant (you may want to digress or flag it as something worth returning to later) or whether it is to be bypassed promptly.

Chip-on-the-shoulder

This is the sort of person who has a pet gripe or who feels

hard done by in some way. Whether the grievance is justified or not, the meeting may not be the place to pursue something that may be a separate issue.

Solution Find out whether the gripes, especially unspecific ones, conceal a real point. Ask the person to be specific. Refer back to the purpose of the meeting: 'Will this help us to …?' Use the group (and time) to confirm the need to concentrate. Promise – if appropriate – to come back to the sore point on another occasion, but get the conversation back on track.

The devious

There is, let us be honest, sometimes rather a lot of deviousness about. There are also many reasons for people not to say exactly what they really feel or mean. These can range from simple fear of losing face to concern with long-term strategy. What people say may underplay, overstate, or disguise the facts, even to the point of sometimes being, let us say, economical with the truth.

Solution Here the good meeting operator learns to read between the lines. Unless you recognise that something beyond the meeting's objectives and content is going on it is difficult, if not impossible, to deal with. The options here vary widely. Sometimes longer-term issues need to be taken forward in parallel with immediate ones. Sometimes deviousness must simply be stamped on, openly and firmly.

The aggressive bully

Some people will ride roughshod over everything, including rules and normal behaviour, to achieve their aim. There may be many reasons: desperation overbalancing discretion, perhaps.

Solution This needs firm action taken without delay (do not wait to 'see if it gets better') and made to stick. Lay down the rules, lay down the law, and use the group to back you up. Being in the chair carries responsibility, and may well demand clout on occasions.

The above examples illustrate the complexity of 'people issues'. Sensitivity to these is always necessary. Sometimes they do not cause great problems; sometimes the solution is found by playing one person off against another (for example, getting a member of the team to 'squash' the talkative person) or by pairing people off (sitting a silent person next to someone able and willing to take time to encourage them); but sometimes – if they are not addressed – these issues can run the meeting into a siding or derail it completely. Although some of the action identified here falls most naturally on whoever is in the chair, everyone can assist if they take a constructive view and act to help make things go well.

What's next?

So, we bear all this in mind, from preparation to conclusion and dealing with awkward participants, and then it is all over and we can get back to work – can't we?

Not yet. Any consideration of making meetings work has to take a broader view than that. So next we turn to what happens *after* meetings.

5 after meetings

The key thing after a meeting is that the actions decided upon should be implemented – as intended and on time, so that the meeting will have been worthwhile. This may involve anything, from a small piece of information being passed on, to the implementation of a major project. Whatever it is, however, it may well need prompting.

Do you need minutes?

This is a question that needs to be asked. There is more than sufficient paperwork in most organisations without encouraging more unless it is truly necessary. So, in some cases the answer will be 'No'. In others some sort of simple written action reminder will be worthwhile. In yet others, where a number of items has been reviewed and there needs to be both an action reminder and a record, then minutes should be prepared. Why? There are three reasons. Minutes provide:

- a prompt to action, reminding those who have taken on, or been given, tasks that they should do them – and do them on time. This may also facilitate liaison when several people are involved in an overlapping way.

- a tangible link to follow-up discussions or a further meeting. This can help ensure that points are reported or taken further. At a subsequent meeting such points often appear under the item 'matters arising'.
- a record of what has occurred and particularly of what decisions were made and what action was decided upon. This may merely be a convenience, a reminder if necessary as time goes by, or it may form an important and permanent record of events, though doubtless you already have enough in your filing systems to make it worthwhile considering carefully how much more you keep, and for how long.

The rule for minutes is straightforward: do not have them unless they are necessary, but do not risk inaction for want of a reminder.

Making them useful

Minutes should not be a chore. They should not be an excuse to write at length, recording every word spoken and every aside too (though the asides may sometimes be the interesting bit). To keep them practical, make minutes or any kind of action-note:

- *accurate*. This may seem obvious but it is important if arguments are to be prevented in future – so no sloppiness or omissions, especially of key points!
- *objective*. The job of whoever prepares these notes is to

report what truly happened, not their embellished view of it.

- *succinct*. Unless they are manageable, the minutes are likely to remain unread – 'brief but encompassing the key points' is the rule.
- *understandable*. Avoid gobbledegook or again the minutes will either remain unread or confuse the issue.
- *business-like*. Their key role is to make it clear *what* action is expected, *by whom* and *when*.

See the minutes as a document that has a specific and important role, yet needing to *earn* a reading, and they are more likely to prove useful.

Format and layout

You may want to follow a planned set of headings. Indeed there may be merit in having all such notes standardised around an organisation, making them easier to prepare and to read. Such standardisation must reflect the needs of those originating it. However, there may well be certain standard features that are worth a comment:

- *apologies/attendance*. It may well be useful to know who was, or was not, present.
- *minutes of the last meeting*. These can be important when the meeting is one of a series.

- *matters arising*. As necessary.
- *items discussed*. Here the relevant facts and decisions are reported rather than a blow-by-blow report of the whole discussion). A reporting style is usually best – 'it was agreed that …' – as this avoids any tendency to list what might or should have happened.

This can be followed by such additional items as 'Any other business' and administrative matters such as the date of a further meeting.

Once the minutes have been prepared, the next question is who should receive a copy. This may necessarily and usefully include a wider circle than that which attended the meeting, but remember not to overwhelm people with paper: ecological considerations apart, there is more than enough to read in most organisations without someone constantly boosting the quantity still more.

The format for such notes is also important. Dense text is to be avoided. They should facilitate the way they will be used – as an *aide-mémoire* at another meeting perhaps, or as a document that will be annotated. The key things that should jump out from the layout are:

- decisions made
- actions to be taken
- who is involved

- the form of those actions
- dates and timing.

The following example makes this clear using three columns.

It was decided that a plan would be developed to show the timings and stages of the project: to be circulated before the next meeting.	**ACTION** P. F. to prepare the necessary plan.	**DATE** To be circulated by 19 August.

Finally, do resolve to write (or get written) the minutes promptly. This is important for several reasons. First, you are more likely to remember the details and remember them accurately. Secondly, people may wait for the minutes before proceeding to actions they must take. And thirdly, prompt action appears more efficient, which may be the right impression to make after the meeting.

Summary

Good meetings do not just happen. That much at least should be clear if you have read this far. But so should the fact that good meetings are possible, and so are meetings that achieve great things. It is never 'just a meeting'. Think what you want to achieve, aim high, manage the detail, and all really can go well.

And now, any other business? Yes: an important point – never end a meeting with the ubiquitous 'AOB (any other business)'. This can jeopardise even the best-run meeting. As you come towards the end, and everyone is expecting to get away, suddenly the chairperson is heard to say, '... and just a few items of AOB ...'. The meeting then nosedives into a mess of bits and pieces, gripes and irrelevances, and people leave irritated. The impact of a good meeting is lost.

It can work well to *start* with AOB: 'Let's take 10 minutes to get a few points out of the way quickly, then we can get down to business.' Remember that although AOB items can be requested in advance or on the day, they do not have to be included; too many meetings contain items that are of importance only to a couple of people, and that would be better dealt with between the two of them on another occasion.

Some meetings are necessarily routine; others are important and should serve to inject enthusiasm and commitment for courses of action discussed.

So, where appropriate, end with a bang and send people away not with the AOB gripes as the last item, but on a high note.

What's next?

That's it. There is a check-list (about procedure) to finish with, but the intention has been to stimulate thinking in a way that helps make your next meeting more interesting, more constructive, and more likely to achieve its objectives.
What are your objectives for *your* next meeting?

appendix

Procedure

Meetings need to be disciplined, though not so much (as we have seen) as to stifle debate and creativity. Perhaps, therefore, the best rule is that there should be as few rules as necessary, or as the circumstances allow (some meetings are constituted in such a way that more are indeed necessary, as for example with an association).

That said, there certainly are some guidelines that may be worth bearing in mind; draw on these as appropriate to help keep your meetings running smoothly and constructively. Here are a few general suggestions first. You might wish to specify:

- the length of notice necessary to call a meeting (and also exactly who can initiate it)
- where and when it is acceptable to hold it (meetings called for a Sunday and scheduled in inaccessible places have been known as a means to reduce attendance and voting)
- the form and style of agendas, and also when they should be prepared and circulated; the same applies to the tabling of reports to be considered by the meeting

- the role of the chairperson (obeying rules, making comments only through the chair etc) as well as who it is – some committees rotate the role (a sensible idea only if it goes to people able to do a competent job)
- language – for example, no raised voices or swearing
- that people declare individual interests.

You may think of more issues relevant to your own situation. You may also have to watch out for legal matters (eg employment legislation in certain kinds of staff meetings).

Greater formality

Where more formality is necessary there is a number of key factors to consider, any of which might on occasion be important to you.

Quorums

At some meetings the number of people attending is important. If a quorum is required then decisions cannot be made without a specified representative number (of whatever whole) being present. A committee may need, say, 50 per cent present to be able to take matters further. Different percentages may apply to different topics. Routine decisions are no problem, but if we are going to vote to blow the entire budget on a trip to Miami then everyone needs to agree! There are clearly occasions where rules in this area are sensible and can prevent problems.

Motions

This is simply a form of words intended to stand on the record. They are used:

- to start a discussion
- after a discussion, to summarise and agree action.

Motions may need to be tabled in advance, proposed and seconded formally, dealt with before the meeting moves on, and voted on to make them firm. The way in which this is to work on a particular occasion must be clear to all concerned, preferably in advance. The wording of motions must be done with some care so that it is clear, positive, and unambiguous.

Amendments

These add to or subtract from a motion or change it in some other way. Formal meetings may need amendments, as well as motions, to be proposed and seconded. There are two types of amendment:

- constructive, which add to the case and are acceptable to the view expressed in the original motion
- wrecking, which are designed to change the whole basis of discussion.

Either must be dealt with before the original motion can be adopted or rejected.

Voting

This can take the form of a simple show of hands, or be more complex – and confidential – involving, say, a ballot paper. However it is done, the procedure and the result should be absolutely clear, be recorded, and must not then be the basis for renewed argument.

Points of order/information

These are interjections to the formal proceedings of the meeting, the first used to indicate a breach of agreed rules, the second to correct something said that is *factually* incorrect.

Overall, rules should be regarded as a means to an end. They are only to be recommended if they help to ensure objectives are met and the meeting goes smoothly and does its job well. Bureaucracy, after all, can all too easily take over, assuming more importance than the real purpose of the meeting. It was inherent in Parkinson's Law that the man who is denied the opportunity to make important decisions begins to regard as important the decisions he is allowed to take. This is a fitting warning with which to end a review designed to focus, above all, on the constructive role of well-run meetings.

With over 90,000 members, the **Institute of Personnel and Development** is the largest organisation in Europe dealing with the management and development of people. The IPD operates its own publishing unit, producing books and research reports for human resource practitioners, students, and general managers charged with people management responsibilities.

Currently there are over 160 titles covering the full range of personnel and development issues. The books have been commissioned from leading experts in the field and are packed with the latest information and guidance to best practice.

For free copies of the IPD Books Catalogue, please contact the publishing department:

Tel.: 0181-263 3387
Fax: 0181-263 3850
E-mail: publish@ipd.co.uk
Web: http://www.ipd.co.uk

Orders for books should be sent to:

Plymbridge Distributors
Estover
Plymouth
Devon
PL6 7PZ

(Credit card orders) Tel.: 01752 202 301
Fax: 01752 202 333

Upcoming titles in the *Management Shapers* series

All titles are priced £5.95 (£5.36 to IPD members)

Body Language at Work

Adrian Furnham

If we know how to send out the right body signals, we can open all sorts of doors for ourselves at work. If we get it wrong, those doors will be slammed in our faces. Body Language at Work explores how and why people communicate their attitudes, emotions and personalities in non-verbal ways.

The book examines:

- the nature and meaning of signals
- why some personalities are easy to read and others difficult
- what our appearance, clothes and mannerisms say about us
- how to detect office liars and fakes.

1999 96 pages ISBN 0 85292 771 1

Introducing NLP

Sue Knight

The management phenomenon of the decade, neuro-linguistic programming (NLP) provides the techniques for personal growth. Use it to develop your credibility potential and value while also learning to excel at communication and interpersonal skills.

The author looks at:

- the essence of NLP and how it can work for you
- using NLP to achieve what you really want
- how to build quality relationships and enhance your influence in the workplace.

1999 96 pages ISBN 0 85292 772 X

Learning for Earning

Eric Parsloe and Caroline Allen

Today, lifelong learning is a must if you want to get onwards and upwards, and if you don't take charge of your own learning, then, frankly, no one else will. Learning for Earning shows exactly how to set about doing this.

The authors examine:

- using interactive exercises, quizzes and games to get you thinking
- how to reflect on what you have read and relate it to your own situation
- how to use other sources of information - people, organisations - to help you
- the use and benefits of 'action promises' - the actions you intend to take after reading.

1999 96 pages ISBN 0 85292 774 6

Other titles in the *Management Shapers* series

All titles are priced at £5.95 (£5.36 to IPD members)

The Appraisal Discussion

Terry Gillen

Shows you how to make appraisal a productive and motivating experience for all levels of performer. It includes:

- assessing performance fairly and accurately
- using feedback to improve performance
- handling reluctant appraisees and avoiding bias
- agreeing future objectives
- identifying development needs.

1998 96 pages ISBN 0 85292 751 7

Asking Questions

Ian MacKay

Will help you ask the 'right' questions, using the correct form to elicit a useful response. All managers need to hone their questioning skills, whether interviewing, appraising or simply exchanging ideas. This book offers guidance and helpful advice on:

- using various forms of open question – including probing, simple interrogative, opinion-seeking, hypothetical, extension and precision etc
- encouraging and drawing out speakers through supportive statements and interjections
- establishing specific facts through closed or 'direct' approaches
- avoiding counter-productive questions
- using questions in a training context.

1998 96 pages ISBN 0 85292 768 1

Assertiveness

Terry Gillen

Will help you feel naturally confident, enjoy the respect of others and easily establish productive working relationships, even with 'awkward' people. It covers:

- understanding why you behave as you do and, when that behaviour is counter-productive, knowing what to do about it
- understanding other people better
- keeping your emotions under control
- preventing others' bullying, flattering or manipulating you
- acquiring easy-to-learn techniques that you can use immediately
- developing your personal assertiveness strategy.

1998 96 pages ISBN 0 85292 769 X

Constructive Feedback

Roland and Frances Bee

Practical advice on when to give feedback, how best to give it, and how to receive and use feedback yourself. It includes:

- using feedback in coaching, training, and team motivation
- distinguishing between criticism and feedback
- 10 tools of giving constructive feedback
- dealing with challenging situations and people.

1998 96 pages ISBN 0 85292 752 5

The Disciplinary Interview

Alan Fowler

This book will ensure that you adopt the correct procedures, conduct productive interviews and manage the outcome with confidence. It includes:

- understanding the legal implications
- investigating the facts and presenting the management case
- probing the employee's case and diffusing conflict
- distinguishing between conduct and competence
- weighing up the alternatives to dismissal.

1998 96 pages ISBN 0 85292 753 3

Leadership Skills

John Adair

Will give you confidence and guide and inspire you on your journey from being an effective manager to becoming a leader of excellence. Acknowledged as a world authority on leadership, Adair offers stimulating insights into:

- recognising and developing your leadership qualities
- acquiring the personal authority to give positive direction and the flexibility to embrace change
- acting on the key interacting needs – to achieve your task, build your team, and develop its members
- transforming the core leadership functions such as planning, communicating and motivating into practical skills you can master.

1998 96 pages ISBN 0 85292 764 9

Listening Skills

Ian MacKay

Improve your ability in this crucial management skill! Clear explanations will help you:

- recognise the inhibitors to listening
- listen to what is really being said by analysing and evaluating the message
- interpret tone of voice and non-verbal signals.

1998 80 pages ISBN 0 85292 754 1

Motivating People

Iain Maitland

Will help you maximise individual and team skills to achieve personal, departmental and, above all, organisational goals. It provides practical insights into:

- becoming a better leader and co-ordinating winning teams
- identifying, setting and communicating achievable targets
- empowering others through simple job improvement techniques
- encouraging self-development, defining training needs and providing helpful assessment
- ensuring that pay and workplace conditions make a positive contribution to satisfaction and commitment.

1998 96 pages ISBN 0 85292 766 5

Negotiating, Persuading and Influencing

Alan Fowler

Develop the skills you need to manage your staff effectively, bargain successfully with colleagues or deal tactfully with superiors. Sound advice on:

- probing and questioning techniques
- timing your tactics and using adjournments
- conceding and compromising to find common ground
- resisting manipulative ploys
- securing and implementing agreement.

1998 96 pages ISBN 085292 755 X

Working in Teams

Alison Hardingham

Looks at teamworking from the inside. It will give you valuable insights into how you can make a more positive and effective contribution – as team member or team leader – to ensure that your team works together and achieves together. Clear and practical guidelines are given on:

- understanding the nature and make-up of teams
- finding out if your team is on track
- overcoming the most common teamworking problems
- recognising your own strengths and weaknesses as a team member
- giving teams the tools, techniques and organisational support they need.

1998 96 pages ISBN 0 85292 767 3